BARBECUE SIDES

Perfect Slaws, Salads, and Snacks for Your Next Cookout

Adam Perry Lang

with Peter Kaminsky

ARTISAN | NEW YORK

Contents

Introduction

A shared meal strengthens familial ties, cements friendships, repairs enmities, establishes sacred communion. Food, family, friendship: they all go together. Just like Thanksgiving and Academy Awards night, a barbecue meal is an occasion for people to gather and bond.

But few books or menus seriously consider the question "Isn't the company you provide for the meat, fish, or fowl on the plate equally important to the success of the meal?" Instead, most people spend hours getting the main course ready, then pile on the baked beans, potato salad, and coleslaw at the last minute and leave it at that. The side dishes are usually an afterthought, when they should be costars. A first-rate barbecue dinner requires that equal care and attention be given to everything that is served with the meat.

Think about what's typically on your plate at a barbecue. Let's say that you have some pulled pork, some baked beans, and some coleslaw. Nobody starts by eating all the meat and, when that is done, eating all the beans and then polishing off the coleslaw. You push some meat onto your fork, then a few sweet and hearty beans and some crunchy, creamy coleslaw, and you taste all three at once. Contrasting tastes and textures make that forkful interesting.

You may recognize some of the recipes in this book as new approaches to old favorites, while others are original creations. One thing you will not find here is the dutiful "serve with" suggestion after each recipe. A plate with barbecue on it requires three items: you pick them. How you put together your ensemble depends on what you are in the mood for. Satisfying spontaneous desire is a much better route than satisfying the instructions in a one-combination-fits-all cookbook suggestion.

It goes without saying that these recipes don't exhaust all the fantastic dishes you can serve at a barbecue, but the principles behind each group can lead to endless variations. As chefs do, let the best items in the markets work on your imagination, and then start chopping and slicing.

MELTING, CREAMY, AND CRISPY

The powerful flavors that are the goal of every griller can easily overwhelm your palate. In order to fully appreciate the main dish, you need some contrasts in texture or temperature. The smooth and creamy dishes in this chapter balance the barbecue without getting in the way of flavor. In addition to tempering the mouthfeel of big, brawny barbecue recipes, these costars can add an unctuous quality that completes lean dishes such as fish or beef or pork tenderloin. And who doesn't love the combination of crispy, salty, and hot? Think about it. You can imagine barbecue without coleslaw, or baked beans, or macaroni and cheese. But no french fries, or crispy fried anything? Does not compute.

MUSHROOMS IN PARSLEY CREAM

SERVES 6 TO 8

Parsley's flavor and texture pair well with anything that has that special "fifth taste" known as umami, which we find in mushrooms, a particularly fine partner for all kinds of meat. This happy pairing has something to do with the texture of cooked mushrooms: smooth and moist, just like the collagen in meat when it has been lovingly cooked for a long time at the right temperature.

Note the use of beurre manié—butter kneaded with flour. It adds enough "stick" to sauces to hold them together without overreducing.

3 tablespoons unsalted butter

1 cup finely chopped shallots

2 garlic cloves, crushed and peeled

Sea or kosher salt and freshly ground white pepper

Juice of 1 lemon, or to taste

2 tablespoons dry white wine

6 cups small firm white button mushrooms

A sprig of fresh thyme

1 cup chicken stock or canned low-sodium broth

2 cups heavy cream

½ teaspoon thinly shaved frozen beurre manié (see Note)

2 tablespoons finely chopped fresh flat-leaf parsley

Cut 2 tablespoons of the butter into ⅓-inch cubes and refrigerate. Heat the remaining 1 tablespoon butter in a 4-quart pot over medium heat until it bubbles gently. Add the shallots, garlic, and a pinch each of salt and white pepper and cook until the shallots are just translucent, 2 to 3 minutes.

Add the lemon juice and white wine, bring to a boil, and cook until most of the liquid has evaporated, 2 to 3 minutes. Add the mushrooms and thyme, stirring well, then add the chicken stock, bring to a boil, and cook until reduced by half.

(continued)

Add the cream, bring to a simmer, and cook for 2 minutes. Add the beurre manié, stirring until incorporated, and simmer very gently for 10 minutes, or until well thickened.

Meanwhile, wrap the parsley in a double layer of cheesecloth, run under cold water, and squeeze dry (rinsing the parsley will cause some of the chlorophyll to leach out and prevent it from giving the cream a greenish tinge).

Taste the mushrooms and adjust the seasoning if necessary. Swirl in the cubed butter piece by piece until incorporated, then remove the pot from the heat and stir in the parsley. Adjust the acidity with a little more lemon juice if necessary, and serve.

Note: *To make beurre manié, blend ⅓ cup all-purpose flour with 8 tablespoons (1 stick) unsalted butter, softened. Transfer to an airtight container, or shape into a log and wrap in plastic wrap and then foil, and freeze until needed. The butter will keep for at least a month.*

FRIED SHALLOT LOAF

SERVES 8 TO 10

While there are a million recipes that start with the instruction "chop the shallots and sauté until golden," there are too few that focus on this relative of garlic and onions. The oniony flavor and aroma of shallots seem to caress every iota of flavor in grilled food, especially meat. They bring out sweetness and savoriness simultaneously. Batter-fried crispness punches it all home.

Vegetable oil for deep-frying
5 cups all-purpose flour
1 tablespoon garlic salt
2½ pounds shallots (about 20 shallots), sliced ⅛ inch thick and separated into rings

1 quart milk
3 large eggs, lightly beaten
Sea or kosher salt

Preheat the oil to 350°F in a deep fryer (see Note). Meanwhile, combine the flour and garlic salt in a large bowl and mix well. Put the shallots in a medium bowl and pour the milk and eggs over them, stirring to combine.

Gently lift out the shallot rings a handful at a time, with some of the milk and egg clinging to them, and toss with the seasoned flour; the shallots will be a bit sticky and clumpy. Put the fryer basket into the fryer, drop in all the floured shallots in an even layer, and immediately put a second fryer basket on top to compress the shallots and submerge them in the oil. Fry until golden brown, 3 to 4 minutes. Carefully remove the shallots from the basket and drain briefly on paper towels, then transfer to a rack and season with salt. Serve immediately.

Note: *If you don't have a deep fryer and two fryer baskets, heat 3 inches of oil in a large, deep pot and cook the shallots in batches, adding them in clumps to the hot oil to make free-form "cakes," or fritters.*

CREAMED CORN WITH CHIVES AND CHILES

SERVES 6 TO 8

Employing cream cheese as a thickener is a surprising use of a familiar taste. People always smile when they figure out that the secret ingredient is something they have eaten and enjoyed their whole lives.

Using the well-known and fondly remembered is a great strategy for creating recipes that people are predisposed to like. It's a door that opens out onto the pleasure in other less familiar ingredients and combinations.

4 tablespoons unsalted butter	4 cups corn kernels (from 7 to 8 ears)
½ cup finely diced Spanish onion	1 cup heavy cream
¼ cup finely diced red bell pepper	4 ounces cream cheese
¼ cup finely diced green bell pepper	Sea or kosher salt and freshly ground white pepper
3 garlic cloves, crushed and peeled	½ cup shredded mild cheddar cheese
1 teaspoon fresh thyme leaves	2 tablespoons thinly sliced (on the bias) scallions
1 teaspoon fresh rosemary leaves	3 tablespoons thinly sliced mild red chile pepper, such as Anaheim
½ teaspoon cayenne pepper	2 tablespoons finely chopped fresh chives
Juice of 1 lemon, or to taste	
1 cup chicken stock or canned low-sodium broth	

Cut 2 tablespoons of the butter into ⅓-inch cubes and refrigerate. Heat the remaining 2 tablespoons butter in a medium saucepan over medium heat until it crackles. Add the onion, bell peppers, garlic, thyme, rosemary, and cayenne and cook, stirring occasionally, until the onion is just translucent, 3 to 4 minutes.

Add the lemon juice and cook until most of the liquid has evaporated, about 1 minute. Add the chicken stock, bring to a boil, and cook until reduced by half.

Add the corn kernels, bring to a simmer, and cook until tender, about 5 minutes.

Meanwhile, bring the cream just to a boil in a small saucepan. Add the cream cheese and whisk gently until melted and smooth.

Add the cream mixture to the corn and stir gently until thoroughly incorporated, then simmer very gently for 3 to 4 minutes, stirring constantly. Season with salt and white pepper, then swirl in the cubed butter piece by piece until incorporated. Stir in the shredded cheese.

Remove from the heat and stir in the scallions, chile, and chives. Add more lemon juice and/or salt and pepper to taste and serve.

BUBBLING BACON BUTTER BEANS

SERVES 6 TO 8

Butter beans are just another name for lima beans, especially in the South. But when they are cooked just right, these beans achieve a state of melty smoothness that is best described by the word *buttery*. In the process of cooking, they throw off starch—just like arborio rice does in risotto. The result is velvety creaminess. The recommendation for these beans is "Serve with anything," because they go with everything. But you could also say, "Serve with nothing else," because they are satisfying all by themselves and quite irresistible when you take them from the oven— steaming, bubbling, and fragrant.

3 tablespoons extra-virgin olive oil, plus more for drizzling

6 slices thick-sliced bacon, cut into 1/4-inch-wide strips

1/2 cup finely chopped shallots

4 garlic cloves, crushed and peeled, plus 1 tablespoon grated garlic (use a Microplane) or garlic mashed to a paste

1 tablespoon chopped fresh sage

2 cups chicken stock or canned low-sodium broth

4 cups cooked butter beans or two 15-ounce jars or cans butter beans, drained, rinsed if canned

1 cup Pomì diced tomatoes (or other Tetra Pak tomatoes), drained

1 teaspoon dried oregano

1/4 cup finely diced prosciutto fat (or additional bacon)

Sea or kosher salt and freshly ground black pepper

2 tablespoons finely chopped fresh flat-leaf parsley

White wine vinegar

Preheat the oven to 300°F.

Heat 2 tablespoons of the olive oil in a large saucepan over medium heat until it sizzles when a piece of bacon is added. Add the rest of the bacon, the shallots, crushed garlic, and sage and cook, stirring, until the shallots are just translucent, 3 to 4 minutes.

(continued)

Add the chicken stock and bring to a boil. Add the beans, bring to a simmer, and simmer for 10 minutes.

Meanwhile, heat the remaining 1 tablespoon olive oil in a small skillet over high heat until very hot. Add the tomatoes and sauté for 2 minutes, then add the grated garlic and oregano and cook until most of the moisture has evaporated and the tomatoes are crackling.

Stir the tomatoes into the bean mixture, along with the prosciutto fat. Season with salt and pepper and pour into a 2-quart casserole or baking dish.

Transfer to the oven and bake for 20 minutes, until the beans are velvety and creamy. If the beans start to look dry, add a splash of water.

Stir the parsley into the beans, adjust the acidity with vinegar as necessary, and drizzle generously with olive oil. Serve, or keep warm in a low oven until ready to serve.

UKBB
(UNITED KINGDOM BAKED BEANS)

SERVES 6 TO 8

Everyone likes baked beans. The English discovered this longtime American staple after World War I, when meat was hard to come by. Baked beans on toast became the go-to solution for a rib-sticking but economical meal. They're still a hallowed element of an English "full monty breakfast," alongside fried eggs (usually cooked in lard), fried tomatoes, and some back bacon. Like the American version, these beans have a tomato-based sauce, but they are less sweet and thick. They are more savory, with a light smokiness, so that their flavor doesn't dominate other dishes on your plate. Instead, they are a smooth complement.

3 tablespoons vegetable oil

6 slices bacon

½ cup finely diced Spanish onion

6 garlic cloves, finely chopped

1 tablespoon onion powder

1 tablespoon garlic salt

½ teaspoon ground cloves

½ teaspoon ground allspice

Sea or kosher salt and freshly ground black pepper

4 cups cooked white kidney beans or two 15-ounce jars or cans white kidney beans, drained, rinsed if canned

1 cup chicken stock or canned low-sodium broth

3 tablespoons light brown sugar

1 cup ketchup

3 tablespoons white wine vinegar

¼ cup finely chopped fresh flat-leaf parsley

2 tablespoons cold unsalted butter, cut into ½-inch cubes

Preheat the oven to 225°F.

Heat the oil in an ovenproof 4-quart pot over medium heat. Add the bacon, onion, garlic, onion powder, garlic salt, cloves, and allspice, season with

salt and pepper, and cook, stirring, until the onion is translucent and the spices are fragrant, 3 to 5 minutes.

Add the beans and chicken stock, bring to a simmer, and simmer for 10 minutes.

Stir in the brown sugar, ketchup, and vinegar and bring back to a simmer. Cover, transfer to the oven, and cook for 1 hour. If the beans seem dry, thin slightly with water.

Set the pot over low heat and stir in the parsley. Swirl in the butter piece by piece until incorporated. Serve, or keep warm in a low oven until ready to serve.

SMOKED-CORN FLAN

SERVES 6 TO 8

Here we have the very essence of "cornness." In the same way that a glass of fresh-squeezed orange juice gives you the pure flavor of two or three oranges, this custard packs in the sweet and savory flavor of half a dozen ears of corn. Setting it in a water bath in the smoker makes for very gentle and even cooking. Cream is flavoristically porous: it picks up smoke in a smoothly sweet way. You will find this flan well suited to fish. Then, if you want a totally contrasting texture, finish the plate with some Crispy Moonshine Onion Rings (page 39).

3 tablespoons unsalted butter, 1 tablespoon softened

2 tablespoons finely chopped shallots

1 tablespoon finely chopped garlic

1 tablespoon chipotle pepper flakes

3 cups corn kernels (from 5 to 6 ears)

Sea or kosher salt and freshly ground black pepper

2 cups heavy cream

2 cups milk

6 large eggs

3 large egg yolks

1 tablespoon fresh thyme leaves

2 tablespoons finely chopped fresh chives

Extra-virgin olive oil for drizzling

Preheat a smoker to 275°F. Butter a 2-quart baking dish with the softened butter.

Melt the remaining 2 tablespoons butter in a 4-quart pot over medium heat. Add the shallots, garlic, chipotle flakes, and corn and cook, stirring, until the shallots are translucent, 2 to 3 minutes. Season with salt and pepper, cover, and cook until the corn is tender, 4 to 5 minutes. Set aside to cool.

Whisk together the cream, milk, eggs, and egg yolks in a large bowl. Add the cooled corn mixture, stirring to combine.

(continued)

Pour the corn mixture into the buttered baking dish and set the dish in a larger baking pan. Add enough hot water to the baking pan to come halfway up the sides of the baking dish and carefully transfer to the smoker. Cook and smoke for 30 minutes.

Sprinkle the flan with the thyme, return to the smoker, and smoke for another 15 minutes, or until just set in the center.

Sprinkle the flan with the chopped chives and drizzle with olive oil. Allow to rest for at least 15 minutes, and up to 1 hour, before serving.

SCRUFFED CARBONARA POTATOES

Think linguine carbonara, only you can eat it with a spoon. Better yet, think gnocchi, but way easier. Instead of making a traditional potato dough, you trim the potatoes into bite-size pieces. The sauce provides all the flavor. Just as with pasta carbonara, the serving bowl is preset with the sauce ingredients. The potatoes have enough residual heat to meld them perfectly. And scruffing the potatoes (see box) makes for a very clingable surface for the sauce.

3 pounds Yukon Gold potatoes, peeled and cut into 1½-inch pieces

Sea or kosher salt

½ cup extra-virgin olive oil, or as needed

4 tablespoons unsalted butter

9 slices bacon, finely chopped

12 garlic cloves, crushed and peeled

2 tablespoons fresh thyme leaves

1 tablespoon fresh rosemary leaves

SAUCE

1 cup extra-virgin olive oil

½ cup clarified butter (see Note), melted and still warm

6 large egg yolks, beaten

Sea or kosher salt and freshly ground black pepper

3 to 4 tablespoons freshly squeezed lemon juice

¾ cup freshly grated Pecorino Romano

¼ cup finely chopped fresh flat-leaf parsley

Put the potatoes in a 4-quart pot with cold water to cover, add 1 tablespoon salt, and bring to a boil over high heat. Reduce the heat to a gentle simmer and cook until the potatoes are just tender, about 10 minutes.

Drain the potatoes in a metal colander, reserving ¼ cup of the potato water, and allow the steam to dissipate for 5 minutes. Toss the potatoes in the colander and allow to stand for 5 minutes longer.

(continued)

Begin to scruff the potatoes by shaking the colander vigorously from side to side about 15 times. Flip the potatoes and give them another 15 shakes.

Put ¼ cup olive oil and 2 tablespoons butter in each of two nonstick skillets that are large enough to hold the potatoes in one layer and heat over medium-high heat until foaming. Add half the potatoes to each pan and cook, without stirring, for 6 minutes. Toss the potatoes and cook for 6 minutes longer, or until they are golden brown.

Push the potatoes aside to clear a small space in the center of each pan; if the pan seems dry, add a splash of olive oil and heat until sizzling. Add half the bacon, garlic, thyme, and rosemary to each pan and cook until the herbs are fragrant and the garlic is lightly golden, 2 to 3 minutes. Toss the garlic, bacon, and herbs with the potatoes and cook, stirring occasionally, for 3 to 4 minutes. Transfer to the colander to drain briefly.

THE ART OF SCRUFFING

Scruffing is the process of roughing up the surface of potatoes, meats, or other grilled or panfried savory eats to create all kinds of nooks and crannies for a crust to develop, places where a baste or sauce could cling for extra flavor.

Meanwhile, make the sauce: Mix the oil and warm clarified butter together in a measuring cup or bowl with a spout; set aside.

Combine the egg yolks and the reserved ¼ cup potato water in a large stainless steel bowl, set over a pot of simmering water, and whisk vigorously until the mixture has doubled in volume and has a velvety texture. Immediately remove from the heat, season with salt and pepper, and add the lemon juice to taste. Gradually whisk in the clarified butter and olive oil.

Cover the bottom of a warm platter with the egg sauce and arrange the potatoes on top. Sprinkle with the grated Pecorino, shower with the chopped parsley, and serve.

Note: *To clarify butter, start with at least ½ pound unsalted butter. Melt the butter in a heavy saucepan over low heat, without stirring. Skim off the foam that rises to the top. Slowly pour the clear melted butter into a bowl or other container, leaving the milk solids in the bottom of the pan. Clarified butter keeps for weeks in the refrigerator and can also be frozen.*

MELTING POTATOES

Creamy, steaming potatoes have always been a favorite partner for robust grilled meats. This dish is less calorie rich than potatoes au gratin or scalloped potatoes but as satisfying in every way. You cut the potatoes into rounds and slowly cook them in chicken stock flavored with garlic, thyme, and rosemary. The magic happens when the stock reduces and marries with the starch from the potatoes. It creates a moist, smooth mouthfeel (or, if you will permit a scientific word, viscosity) that has the same sensation as the melted collagen in long-cooked meat like pulled pork, brisket, or leg of lamb. Instead of overstimulating the palate, the potatoes calm it down, which is just what you want to do when serving kick-ass barbecued meat.

2 tablespoons unsalted butter, plus 2 tablespoons cold butter, cut into ½-inch cubes

2 tablespoons extra-virgin olive oil, plus more if necessary

5 to 6 russet (baking) potatoes, peeled, cut into ½-inch-thick slices, and edges trimmed to round them

Sea or kosher salt and freshly ground black pepper

15 garlic cloves, crushed and peeled

1 tablespoon fresh thyme leaves

1 tablespoon fresh rosemary leaves

2 cups chicken stock or canned low-sodium broth

1 cup water

2 tablespoons chopped fresh flat-leaf parsley

Juice of ½ lemon, or to taste

Put 1 tablespoon of the butter and 1 tablespoon of the olive oil in each of two nonstick skillets that are large enough to hold half the potatoes in one layer and heat over medium-high heat until the butter stops crackling. Add half the potatoes to each pan and cook until golden brown on the bottom, about 3 minutes. Flip the potatoes over, season with salt and pepper, and cook until golden brown on the second side, about 3 minutes.

(continued)

Push the potatoes aside to clear a small space in the center of each pan; if the pan seems dry, add a splash of olive oil and heat until sizzling. Add half the garlic, thyme, and rosemary to each pan and cook until fragrant, about 2 minutes. Add half the chicken stock and water to each pan and bring to a boil; reduce the heat to a simmer, cover, and cook until the potatoes are just tender, about 15 minutes.

Remove the lids, raise the heat, and cook until there are just a few tablespoons of liquid remaining in the pans. Remove from the heat and swirl in the cubed butter piece by piece until incorporated, then stir in the parsley. Add a splash of lemon juice, adjust the seasoning, and serve.

POTATO CREAM WITH LEEKS, CAPERS, AND AVOCADO

SERVES 6

If an around-the-world ticket is a little rich for your blood but you find yourself in New York City, hop on the Number 7 subway to Queens. Every stop puts you in a different country: Thailand, Spain, Korea, Uruguay, China, Russia, and more. Queens is a true melting pot, with lots of different foods melting in lots of different pots. Over the last few decades, a number of Colombian restaurants have popped up in the borough to serve that growing immigrant community. And they all serve the dish that inspired this recipe: ajiaco, a potato and chicken stew with herbs and avocado. This version omits the chicken for a side dish that can go with any number of entrees, such as chicken or lightly smoked cod.

2 tablespoons extra-virgin olive oil

1 cup sliced leeks (split the leeks lengthwise first and cut into ¼-inch-thick slices)

½ cup finely chopped Spanish onion

3 garlic cloves, crushed and peeled

Sea or kosher salt and freshly ground black pepper

4 cups ½-inch-dice russet (baking) potatoes

2 cups chicken stock or canned low-sodium broth

2 cups water

1 tablespoon fresh thyme leaves

2 teaspoons dried oregano

¾ cup heavy cream

GARNISHES

¾ cup heavy cream

2 ripe avocados

Generous splash of lemon juice

Sea or kosher salt and freshly ground black pepper

3 tablespoons drained capers

2 tablespoons fresh dill

2 tablespoons chopped fresh chives

2 teaspoons fresh lemon thyme leaves

2 tablespoons extra-virgin olive oil

3 lemons, cut in half

Heat the olive oil in a 4-quart pot over medium-low heat until hot. Add the leeks, onion, and garlic, stir to coat with the oil, and season with a pinch each of salt and pepper. Cover and cook until the onion and garlic are translucent, about 5 minutes.

Add the potatoes, stock, water, thyme, and oregano, season with salt and pepper, and bring to a boil. Reduce the heat to a simmer and cook until the potatoes are tender, 30 to 40 minutes.

Add the cream, bring to a simmer, and cook for 10 minutes longer, or until the potatoes are soft.

Meanwhile, for the garnishes: Whip the cream to semi-firm peaks; refrigerate. Halve, peel, and pit the avocados. Cut into ¼-inch-thick slices and toss with the lemon juice and salt and pepper to taste.

Using an immersion blender, blend the potatoes to a coarse puree; or use a regular blender and pulse just until coarsely pureed, not smooth. The potato cream should have the consistency of a thick soup; if necessary, thin with a little water. Adjust the seasoning if necessary.

Ladle the potato cream onto a deep platter (if topping with grilled meat) or into a serving bowl and swirl in the whipped cream. Scatter the avocado, capers, and herbs over the top, drizzle with the olive oil, and serve with the lemons.

CREAMED SPINACH WITH STEEPED AND SMOKED GARLIC CONFIT

SERVES 8 TO 12

Creamed spinach is a standby in every steak house in America. This version was inspired by the legendary Peter Luger Steak House in Brooklyn's Williamsburg neighborhood. It is the favorite of a lot of New Yorkers, as well as thousands of visitors to the city. By using frozen spinach, you already begin with a soft, almost creamy texture, and you don't have to mask its beautiful green chlorophyll by cooking it forever to soften it. The confited smoked garlic flavors the cream and binds everything together as well as any roux would—and no roux has the deep nutty taste that you get from this garlic confit.

16 garlic cloves, crushed and peeled

1 cup extra-virgin olive oil

1 cup finely diced Spanish onion

1 tablespoon sea or kosher salt, or to taste

1 tablespoon garlic powder

1 tablespoon onion powder

1 tablespoon freshly ground white pepper, or to taste

3 cups heavy cream

4 pounds frozen spinach, defrosted, drained, and squeezed dry (2 pounds drained weight)

6 tablespoons unsalted butter, cut into ½-inch cubes and softened

Preheat a smoker to 275°F.

Combine the garlic and olive oil in a 4-quart baking dish, put it in the smoker, and cook until the garlic is tender and golden, about 1 hour.

Preheat the oven to 300°F.

Transfer the smoked garlic to an 8-quart ovenproof pot, add the onion and salt, and cook over medium-low heat, stirring occasionally, until the onion is translucent.

Add the garlic powder, onion powder, and white pepper, stirring well. Add the heavy cream, bring to a simmer, and simmer for 10 minutes, stirring occasionally.

Remove from the heat and stir in the spinach. Transfer to the oven and cook for 45 minutes, or until the spinach is very tender.

Remove the spinach from the oven and, using an immersion blender, blend until smooth. Add the butter, stirring with a heatproof spatula until it melts. Taste, adjust the seasoning if necessary, and serve.

POLENTA WITH MASCARPONE AND ROSEMARY

SERVES 6 TO 8

If there is one thing that always goes with grilled meat, it's thick, creamy polenta made with rich mascarpone. The mascarpone oozes out of the polenta and then sets up into a thin crust. Rosemary lends a piney note that helps to focus the broad flavors of the cheese and cornmeal.

On a crisp October day, this dish has the stick-to-your-ribs heartiness that you crave after a long trudge through the forest when the leaves are falling and the first frost is on the way.

6 cups milk	3 tablespoons unsalted butter
1 cup heavy cream	1 cup freshly grated Parmesan
3 garlic cloves, crushed and peeled	1/2 cup mascarpone
2 tablespoons fresh rosemary leaves	2 tablespoons fresh marjoram leaves
Sea or kosher salt and freshly ground black pepper	Grated zest of 2 lemons
2 1/2 cups instant polenta	2 tablespoons extra-virgin olive oil

Combine the milk, cream, garlic, rosemary, and salt and pepper to taste in a 4-quart pot and bring just to a boil. Reduce the heat to a lazy simmer and add the polenta in a slow, steady stream, whisking constantly. Cook, stirring frequently, until the polenta is the consistency of thick porridge and smooth.

Remove from the heat, add the butter, Parmesan, and mascarpone, and whisk in, slowly at first and then increasing the pace, until fully incorporated. Taste and adjust the seasoning. The polenta can be served immediately or kept warm for up to 30 minutes.

To serve, transfer the polenta to a platter or serving bowl, sprinkle with the marjoram and lemon zest, and drizzle with the olive oil.

DUCK-FAT FRIES

SERVES 6 TO 8

Frying in olive oil, canola, butter, lard, and all of the industrial super-hydrogenated goo has received justifiably bad press in recent years because it is unhealthful. And all these fats also produce fries that taste blah. Duck fat, on the other hand, creates french-fried potatoes that your friends and family will devour. Note that the Wine Vinegar Salt must be made 14 hours in advance.

3 quarts duck fat

2½ pounds russet (baking) potatoes (8 medium to large potatoes)

2 garlic cloves, grated (use a Microplane)

2 tablespoons olive oil

2 tablespoons finely chopped fresh flat-leaf parsley

1 tablespoon Wine Vinegar Salt (recipe follows)

Heat the duck fat to 325°F in a large pot. Meanwhile, cut the unpeeled potatoes into ¼-inch-thick french fries. Transfer to a colander and rinse under cold water until the water runs clear. Drain, then lightly pat dry with paper towels.

A handful at a time, add the potatoes to the hot fat and cook for 3 minutes to blanch them. Remove with a spider or slotted spoon, transfer to a baking sheet, and allow to cool. Set the pot of oil aside until just before serving time. (You can cook the potatoes to this point up to 3 hours ahead.)

When ready to serve, heat the duck fat to 325°F again. Combine the garlic and olive oil in a small cup.

Working in batches, add the potatoes to the hot fat, without crowding the pot, and fry until golden brown, 3 to 4 minutes. Transfer to a large stainless steel bowl. Scatter the parsley, garlic oil, and wine vinegar salt over the hot fries, tossing to distribute the seasonings evenly, and serve.

Wine Vinegar Salt

The English love salt and vinegar on their potato crisps, or, as Americans call them, potato chips. They are also partial to the same combination on their batter-fried fish. By infusing the vinegar into the salt, you get all the flavor but none of the sogginess that defeats a golden crust. Wine vinegar, rather than cider vinegar or white vinegar, contributes a hint of floral fruit.

1 cup sea or kosher salt
⅓ cup red or white wine vinegar

Combine the salt and vinegar in a bowl, stirring until slushy.

Spread the salt mixture out in a thin, even layer on a parchment-lined dehydrator tray and dry in a dehydrator at 105°F for 12 hours. Alternatively, spread the mixture on a parchment-lined baking sheet, put in a convection oven set at the lowest setting, prop the door ajar with the handle of a wooden spoon, and let dry completely, about 12 hours.

Finely grind in a spice grinder or clean coffee grinder and dry for another 2 hours.

Transfer the salt mixture back to the grinder and pulse to the consistency of sand. Store in an airtight container at room temperature for up to 1 month.

CRISPY MOONSHINE ONION RINGS

SERVES 6 TO 8

It has been known for some time that using vodka—which evaporates quickly—or club soda instead of water makes for less watery batter. David Chang is one of many modern chefs who has used vodka this way. Here moonshine replaces the vodka for a unique twist.

8 cups peanut oil

3 large Spanish onions, cut into ½-inch-thick slices and separated into rings

1 cup milk

2 cups all-purpose flour

2 teaspoons sea or kosher salt, plus more for sprinkling

2 teaspoons freshly ground black pepper

BATTER

4 large egg whites

1 cup The Original Moonshine clear corn whiskey or vodka

2 cups cornstarch

2 teaspoons sea or kosher salt

2 teaspoons freshly ground black pepper

2 teaspoons cayenne pepper

About 4 cups panko crumbs

Heat the oil to 350°F in an 8-quart pot. Meanwhile, put the onions in a large bowl and pour the milk over them to moisten them; drain.

Put the flour in a large sealable plastic bag, add the salt and pepper, and shake to mix. Working in batches, add the drained onion slices to the flour, seal the bag, and shake vigorously to coat the slices, then spread on a baking sheet.

Make the batter: Whip the egg whites to soft peaks in a large bowl. Fold in the moonshine. Sift the cornstarch, salt, black pepper, and cayenne over the egg whites and fold in gently.

Spread the panko crumbs evenly on a second baking sheet. Line another baking sheet with paper towels.

(continued)

Working in batches, add the onion rings to the batter, then, one at a time, toss onto the panko crumbs and flip over to coat with crumbs; repeat until you have filled the baking sheet with a generously spaced layer of onions.

One by one, drop the coated onions into the hot oil, without crowding, and cook until golden brown, 3 to 4 minutes. Remove with a spider or slotted spoon, transfer to the lined baking sheet to drain briefly, and sprinkle with salt, then transfer to a mesh cooling rack (this will prevent the onion rings from becoming soggy). Repeat with the remaining onion rings and serve.

CHICKEN SKIN COOKED
AND CRISPED UNDER A BRICK

SERVES 6 TO 8

Among the handful of universal truths in eating is that it's rare to meet someone who doesn't like crisped chicken skin. If you give a kid a choice between chicken meat and chicken skin, you know they're going to choose the skin. This recipe, in which the skin is hydrated with water, garlic, and herbs and then crisped under a brick, is unbelievably flavorful as well as enjoyably crisp.

2 pounds chicken skin

1 tablespoon Four Seasons Blend (see page 47)

1 teaspoon garlic salt

1 teaspoon freshly ground black pepper

1 tablespoon finely chopped fresh flat-leaf parsley

Preheat the oven to 350°F.

Season the chicken skin with the seasoning blend. Line a baking sheet with a nonstick baking mat or parchment paper and spread the chicken skin on it. Cover with another baking mat or sheet of parchment, set another baking sheet on top, and put a clean brick wrapped in foil on top of the baking sheet to weight it down.

Put the chicken skin in the oven and cook for 20 minutes. Remove from the oven, being mindful of the rendered fat, remove the brick and the top baking sheet and baking mat, and carefully pour off the fat.

Lightly dab the skin with a paper towel and put the baking mat, baking sheet, and brick back on top. Continue to cook, checking after 15 minutes and then every 5 minutes thereafter, until the skin is golden brown and crispy, about 40 minutes in all.

Using tongs, transfer the hot skin to a large bowl and toss with the garlic salt, pepper, and parsley, then immediately transfer to a wire cooling rack. Allow to cool and crisp for 5 minutes, and serve.

SUPER-CRISP PORK RINDS

SERVES 8 TO 10

Pork rinds have finally begun to assume their rightful place in American food culture. Once they were a Southern or Mexican treat, but now everybody loves them. The trick is boiling, baking, and finally frying to super-crispiness.

5 pounds pork skin with rind
(4 sheets approximately 12 by
12 inches and ¼ inch thick)

2 tablespoons sea or kosher salt

1 lemon, cut in half

3 quarts vegetable oil

Four Seasons Blend (see page 47),
for sprinkling

Put the pork skin in a large pot; add the salt and enough water to cover generously. Squeeze each lemon half into the pot and then drop the halves into the water. Bring to a boil over high heat. Reduce to a low boil and cook until the skin is extremely tender, just shy of falling apart, about 3 hours; replenish the water as necessary.

Line a large baking dish with plastic wrap and layer the pork skin in the dish (if it falls apart a bit, just fit it back together again like patchwork). Cover the dish with plastic wrap, place a baking pan that just fits inside the dish on top, and weight with a couple of heavy cans or a brick. Refrigerate for at least 6 hours; the layered skin should be very firm and solid.

Heat the oil to 350°F in a large pot. Meanwhile, remove the weights and top layer of plastic wrap from the baking dish, turn the pork skin out onto a cutting board, and peel off the remaining plastic wrap. Using a meat fork to anchor the skin, cut it into ¼-inch-wide strips with a serrated knife.

Working in batches, add the pork skin to the hot oil (taking care to protect yourself from the popping skin—use a spatter shield if you have

42 | Barbecue Sides

one) and fry for 10 to 12 minutes, until crisp and golden brown. (The pork skin will pop and sizzle at first and then stop crackling—it may seem as if nothing is happening, but it will become tender and crispy in the silent oil.) Remove with a spider or slotted spoon and immediately sprinkle with the seasoning blend. Serve hot, or keep warm in a low oven until ready to serve; or allow to cool and serve at room temperature.

THREE
MEATY CLASSICS

With side dishes this delicious, you could almost forget there was something missing from the table. But when you're hankering for seared meat to accompany your crisp salads and crackling fries, these classic recipes will hit your backyard gathering out of the park. The three recipes in this section reconsider some old favorites in a new light, simplifying and teasing out taste and texture so that they come together as elegantly and clearly as possible.

The techniques that follow are intended to construct a powerful taste narrative, to layer flavor and texture, one after the other, so that each bite is a story with a beginning, middle, and end. And when the story is told, what should stay with you is the quality of the prime ingredient: the meat.

Building flavor begins with seasoning. And you can't go wrong with just salt, black pepper, garlic salt, and cayenne. This is a big departure from the practice of most barbecue chefs, who create complex rubs with celery salt, onion powder, paprika, ground spices, and MSG, in addition to these four.

But that's not the right technique for the way real people—even barbecue judges—eat in the real world. We take some meat, some sauce, and some vegetables, often on the same forkful. This approach calls for balance, not blowout, for the building and mixing of flavors and textures that seduce and ultimately satisfy—which brings us back to the "Four Seasons": salt, black pepper, garlic salt, and cayenne.

Why these four? Salt is the most fundamental taste. Without it, most foods are boring. Salt lifts all other flavors. Black pepper has warmth and a musky aroma. It helps to focus all the broad powerful notes in barbecued food. Garlic salt doesn't burn the way garlic powder does, and it makes flavor punchier. It gives the Four Seasons focus, as well as a dimension of depth and aroma. The spicy heat of cayenne wakes up the other seasonings in any food, and it adds the indefinable but pleasant quality of zing. A painter would say it puts down a base coat that is the foundation of a vibrant mahogany color. It's a signal from your eyes to your brain: "Here comes something delicious, so tell your mouth to start watering."

Four Seasons Blend

MAKES APPROXIMATELY 1 CUP

1 cup sea or kosher salt
2 tablespoons freshly ground black pepper

2 tablespoons garlic salt
1 teaspoon cayenne pepper

Combine the salt, black pepper, garlic salt, and cayenne in a small bowl. Transfer to a spice grinder or clean coffee grinder and pulse to the consistency of sand. Store in an airtight container for up to 1 month.

THE MEAT PASTE

Season the meat all over with the Four Seasons Blend (see previous page) and/or other seasoning. Lightly moisten your hands and work the seasonings into the meat. Let the meat stand for 5 to 10 minutes. Through osmosis, the salt will penetrate the meat and push and pull out flavor components, creating a "meat paste" on the surface. With more delicate flesh—fish, for example—you want to limit the amount of time that you allow this paste to form or you will risk "salt burn."

This paste—the union of the seasonings and juices from the meat—will begin to form a glaze just as soon as you put the meat on the grill or in the smoker. Juices continue to escape from the meat and concentrate in the crust while a basting mixture adds more flavor. It's a win-win situation.

THE HERB BASTING BRUSH

Rather than use an ordinary basting brush, make your own by securing a bunch of herb sprigs (rosemary, sage, or thyme, or a combination—or other herbs, depending on what you are cooking) to a dowel, the handle of a wooden spoon, or a long-handled carving fork. The herb brush flavors the baste, releases

oils into the crust as it builds, and eventually becomes a garnish for the Board Dressing (see below). Plus, it looks really cool and makes people think "Food!" when they see you using it.

THE BOARD DRESSING

Once you have grilled a piece of meat, you want to capture the flavors of the delicious juices that emerge on the cutting board when you slice it and then build upon them. To do so, make a board dressing.

For a basic board dressing, combine 6 tablespoons extra-virgin olive oil, 2 tablespoons finely chopped fresh flat-leaf parsley, and sea or kosher salt and freshly ground black pepper to taste. You can improvise here, adding grated shallots or garlic (use a Microplane), finely chopped chiles, chopped scallions, and/or other chopped herbs, such as rosemary, thyme, and sage.

The secret flavorful last ingredient is the tip of the herb basting brush, chopped very fine and mixed into the dressing. After

being in contact with the hot meat while it cooked, the rosemary, sage, or thyme will have softened a bit and released some aromatic and flavorful oils. Mix the herbs into the board dressing, then slice the meat, turning each slice in the dressing to coat. Then pour the resulting board juices over the meat when you serve it.

MAN STEAK
WITH THYME ZINFANDEL SALT

SERVES 6 TO 8

In England, a very big steak is called a "man steak," no doubt because it is big, like an Englishman's appetite. It's somewhat haphazardly cut to include a few muscles in and around the rump, and it doesn't look like any recognizable steak. When you see a T-bone—or a rib eye or a shell steak—you know what it is right away. With the man steak, the visual is that of an oversize hunk of meat on Fred Flintstone's grill.

This massive mix of muscles makes for a steak with varying textures and tenderness, which is interesting. This recipe is a staple because nothing says barbecue like a beautifully done steak. If you cook it right and baste it lovingly, let it rest, temper, and baste again, the result is an intensely flavorful crust and a juicy, toothsome interior. Note that the Thyme Zinfandel Salt must be made 14 hours in advance.

THYME ZINFANDEL SALT
1 cup sea or kosher salt
⅓ cup zinfandel
1 tablespoon dried thyme

One 6-pound "man steak" (see headnote)
¼ cup Four Seasons Blend (see page 47)
1 tablespoon freshly ground black pepper

BASIC BASTE
1¼ cups extra-virgin olive oil
10 tablespoons (1¼ sticks) unsalted butter
1 tablespoon soy sauce

1 tablespoon granulated sugar
2 tablespoons grated garlic (use a Microplane) or garlic mashed to a paste
1 tablespoon fresh thyme leaves
2 tablespoons grated Spanish onion (use a Microplane)
2 teaspoons sea or kosher salt
2 teaspoons freshly ground black pepper
1 teaspoon red pepper flakes
¼ cup freshly squeezed lemon juice
¼ cup white wine vinegar

An herb brush (see page 48)
Board Dressing (see page 49)

Prepare the Thyme Zinfandel Salt: Combine the salt and wine in a bowl, stirring until slushy. Spread the salt mixture out in a thin, even layer on a parchment-lined dehydrator tray and dry in a dehydrator at 105°F for 12 hours. Alternatively, spread the mixture on a parchment-lined baking sheet, put in a convection oven set at the lowest setting, prop the door ajar with the handle of a wooden spoon, and let dry completely, about 12 hours. Finely grind in a spice grinder or clean coffee grinder and dry for another 2 hours. Transfer the salt mixture back to the grinder, add the dried thyme, and pulse to the consistency of sand. Store in an airtight container at room temperature for up to 1 month.

Preheat the grill to medium-low.

Season the beef all over with the seasoning blend and black pepper, then lightly moisten your hands with water and rub the seasonings into the meat. Allow to stand for 10 minutes to develop a "meat paste" (see page 48).

Meanwhile, prepare the Basic Baste: Combine the olive oil, butter, soy sauce, sugar, garlic, thyme, onion, salt, black pepper, and red pepper flakes in a 2-quart saucepan and bring just to a simmer; remove from the heat. (For the best flavor, refrigerate in a tightly sealed container for 1 to 2 days and reheat over low heat to melt the butter before using.) Whisk the lemon juice and vinegar into the baste before using.

Put the beef on the clean (unoiled) grill grate and cook, without moving it, for 1 minute. Turn, grabbing the bone portion with your tongs, baste with the herb brush, and cook for 1 minute. Turn the steak, baste with the herb brush, and continue to cook, turning the meat every 2 minutes or so and basting each time you flip it, for 17 more minutes. The meat may stick and tear a bit, but this is OK, even desirable—the sticking and tearing is called "scruffing" (see "The Art of Scruffing," page 25). The surface should begin to crust after scruffing. (For newer grills, where less sticking and

Turn, making sure to grab the bone portion with tongs (as in the photo), and baste immediately with the herb brush.

It's big, it's juicy, it has every texture known to steakdom, something to satisfy every steak lover, with plenty more to choose from for the rest of the table. Steak doesn't get more dramatic or imposing.

tearing occur, or for increased surface area, score the steak with a knife.) Transfer the steak to a large platter and allow to rest for 10 minutes.

Meanwhile, clean and oil the grill grate.

Put the steak back on the grill and cook, turning and basting it every 4 minutes, until the internal temperature registers 115°F on an instant-read thermometer for rare, 25 to 35 minutes.

Meanwhile, pour the board dressing onto a cutting board (or mix it directly on the board). Finely chop the tip of the herb brush and mix the herbs into the dressing.

Season the steak on both sides with thyme salt, transfer to the cutting board, and allow to rest for 10 minutes.

To serve, slice the meat ¼ inch thick, turning each slice in the dressing to coat, and arrange on plates. Pour the board juices over the meat and finish with a sprinkling of the thyme salt.

ROASTED RIB STACK WITH WORCESTERSHIRE SALT

SERVES 8 TO 12

By stacking racks of ribs one on top of the other and wrapping them in bacon, you construct a thick "roast" out of three or four thinner cuts. The meat emerges more succulent than single racks of ribs would, infused with a strong smoky, salty, bacony flavor. The stack is smoked for 3 hours, then finished over direct heat. Note that the Worcestershire Salt must be made 14 hours in advance.

WORCESTERSHIRE SALT

1 cup sea or kosher salt

1 cup Worcestershire sauce

1 tablespoon freshly ground black pepper

4 racks St. Louis spareribs (about 2½ pounds each)

6 tablespoons Four Seasons Blend (see page 47)

20 to 30 slices bacon

CLASSIC SOUTHERN BASTE

1¼ cups extra-virgin olive oil

10 tablespoons (1¼ sticks) unsalted butter

1 teaspoon soy sauce

1 teaspoon Worcestershire sauce

1 tablespoon dark brown sugar

2 tablespoons grated garlic (use a Microplane) or garlic mashed to a paste

1 tablespoon fresh thyme leaves

2 tablespoons grated Spanish onion (use a Microplane)

2 teaspoons sea or kosher salt

2 teaspoons freshly ground black pepper

1 teaspoon red pepper flakes

½ cup cider vinegar

1 tablespoon ketchup

1 tablespoon yellow mustard

An herb brush (see page 48)

Board Dressing (see page 49) or BBQ Sauce (recipe follows)

Prepare the Worcestershire Salt: Combine the salt and Worcestershire sauce in a bowl, stirring until slushy. Spread the salt mixture out in a thin, even layer on a parchment-lined dehydrator tray and dry in a dehydrator at 105°F for 12 hours. Alternatively, spread the mixture on a parchment-lined baking sheet, put in a convection oven set at the lowest setting, prop the door ajar with the handle of a wooden spoon, and let dry completely, about 12 hours. Finely grind in a spice grinder or clean coffee grinder and dry for another 2 hours. Transfer the salt mixture back to the grinder, add the pepper, and pulse to the consistency of fine sand. Store in an airtight container at room temperature for up to 1 month.

Season the ribs all over with the seasoning blend. Stack the racks on top of each other, laying a strip of bacon between each layer. Starting at one end, drape a slice of bacon over the entire stack, allowing it to hang down evenly on both sides. Place another slice of bacon next to the first one, overlapping it by ¼ inch. Continue down the entire length of the stack, covering it from end to end. Wrap tightly in plastic wrap and then in heavy-duty aluminum foil and refrigerate for 30 minutes.

Preheat a smoker to 275°F.

Put the wrapped stack round side up on the smoker grate and smoke for 1 hour.

Remove the ribs from the smoker and unwrap. Place back on the smoker, continue to cook for 2 hours, and then remove.

Preheat a grill to medium.

Meanwhile, prepare the Classic Southern Baste: Combine the olive oil, butter, soy sauce, Worcestershire sauce, brown sugar, garlic, thyme, onion, salt, black pepper, and red pepper flakes in a 2-quart saucepan and bring just to a simmer; remove from the heat. (For the best flavor, refrigerate in a tightly sealed container for 1 to 2 days and reheat over low heat to melt the butter before using.)

Remove the bacon from the outside of the rack. Finely chop and set aside to add to the board dressing or sauce. Separate the slabs of ribs (reserving the bacon between the layers as well) and lightly coat with the baste, using the herb brush. Whisk the vinegar, ketchup, and mustard into the remaining baste.

(continued)

Wrapping a stack of ribs in bacon seals in juiciness, adds smoky seasoning, and promotes even roasting. As the ribs cook inside their "bacon envelope," they develop extra-juicy succulence.

Put the racks top side down on the clean (unoiled) grill grate and grill, turning and basting them with the herb brush every 5 minutes or so, until crisp and browned on both sides, about 45 minutes. The meat should be tender but not falling apart.

Meanwhile, pour the board dressing or BBQ sauce onto a cutting board (or mix the dressing directly on the board). If using the dressing, finely chop the tip of the herb brush and mix the herbs into the dressing. Mix the chopped bacon into the dressing or BBQ sauce, if desired.

Season the ribs on both sides with Worcestershire salt and transfer to the cutting board. Cut into individual ribs, turning each rib to coat in the dressing or sauce, and transfer to plates or a platter. Finish with a sprinkling of the Worcestershire salt and serve.

BBQ Sauce

½ cup vegetable oil

5 garlic cloves, crushed and peeled

2 teaspoons garlic salt

1 tablespoon chili powder

1 cup packed light brown sugar

2 cups water

2 cups ketchup

½ cup unsulfured blackstrap molasses

½ cup cider vinegar

1 teaspoon Worcestershire sauce

½ cup yellow mustard

¼ cup red pepper jelly

¼ teaspoon liquid smoke

Combine the oil and garlic in a medium pot and cook over low heat, stirring occasionally, until the garlic is lightly golden, 2 to 3 minutes. Add the garlic salt, chili powder, and brown sugar and cook, stirring constantly, for 1 minute.

Add the water, ketchup, molasses, vinegar, Worcestershire sauce, mustard, pepper jelly, and liquid smoke and bring to a boil. Reduce the heat and simmer gently, stirring frequently to prevent burning, until reduced to 4 cups, 20 to 30 minutes. Remove from the heat and allow to cool. The sauce will keep, refrigerated in an airtight container, for up to 1 week.

SMOKED CRACK-BACK CHICKEN WITH LEMON, GARLIC, AND HERBES DE PROVENCE BASTE

SERVES 4

Ask any French chef worth their toque what their favorite meal is, and the answer will be a perfect roast chicken served with a laboriously prepared sauce. The secret is roasting the bones and caramelizing the juices that are then extracted in the stock-making process. Most home cooks don't go to such lengths. In fact, most restaurant chefs don't either, leaving that task to the lower ranks of their kitchen brigade.

The solution here is to crack the bones of the intact chicken, then stab it repeatedly. The result looks like a chicken that ran into a truck. But by cracking the bones and stabbing, you can smoke the chicken whole and still get the flavor-rich juices from the bones.

Put the bird in a cast-iron pan in a smoker, so that instead of being lost to the coals, the fat, flavor, and juices collect in the bottom of the pan. Then use them to baste and glaze the chicken to produce a crust as deeply flavored and crispy as that of any Parisian pullet. The brine adds flavor, of course, but it also preserves moisture, which is critical to keep the white meat from drying out while the longer-cooking dark meat finishes. Note that the chicken needs to marinate for 24 hours and the Lemon Thyme Salt must be made 14 hours in advance.

LEMON THYME SALT

1 cup sea or kosher salt

1 tablespoon grated lemon zest

⅓ cup freshly squeezed lemon juice

1 tablespoon fresh thyme leaves

One 3½-pound chicken

8 cups Basic Brine or Very Basic Brine (recipes follow)

1 tablespoon Four Seasons Blend (see page 47)

LEMON, GARLIC, AND HERBES DE PROVENCE BASTE

1¼ cups extra-virgin olive oil

10 tablespoons (1¼ sticks) unsalted butter

1 tablespoon granulated sugar

2 tablespoons grated garlic (use a Microplane) or garlic mashed to a paste

2 tablespoons grated Spanish onion (use a Microplane)

1 tablespoon dried oregano

1 tablespoon dried lavender

1 tablespoon fresh rosemary leaves

1 tablespoon fresh thyme leaves

1 tablespoon fresh flat-leaf parsley leaves

2 teaspoons sea or kosher salt

2 teaspoons freshly ground black pepper

1 teaspoon red pepper flakes

An herb brush (see page 48)

¼ cup white wine vinegar

¼ cup freshly squeezed lemon juice

VEGETABLES AND HERBS

½ cup finely chopped shallots

¼ cup finely chopped carrots

¼ cup finely chopped celery

6 bay leaves, preferably fresh

1 tablespoon fresh thyme leaves

½ cup dry white wine

1½ cups chicken stock or canned low-sodium broth

2 tablespoons cold unsalted butter, cut into small cubes

2 tablespoons finely chopped fresh flat-leaf parsley

Prepare the Lemon Thyme Salt: Combine the salt, zest, and juice in a bowl, stirring until slushy. Spread the salt mixture out in a thin, even layer on a parchment-lined dehydrator tray and dry in a dehydrator at 105°F for 12 hours. Alternatively, spread the mixture on a parchment-lined baking sheet, put in a convection oven set at the lowest setting, prop the door ajar with the handle of a wooden spoon, and let dry completely, about 12 hours. Finely grind in a spice grinder or clean coffee grinder and dry for another 2 hours. Transfer the salt mixture back to the grinder, add the thyme, and pulse to the consistency of sand. Store in an airtight container at room temperature for up to 1 month.

Crack the back of the chicken by placing it on its side and pressing down on it. Then, holding the breast, tap and lightly smash the back of the chicken until it feels like a tight bag of marbles. Insert a thin sharp knife into the back of the chicken to make about 10 evenly spaced holes, pushing the knife through the carcass and twisting it.

(continued)

Put the chicken in a large heavy-duty plastic bag or a bowl and add the brine. Seal the bag or cover the bowl and refrigerate for 24 hours.

Put a large cast-iron skillet in a smoker and preheat the smoker to 350°F.

Remove the chicken from the brine (discard the brine) and, while it is still moist, season it all over with the seasoning blend, working it in with your hands. Truss the chicken.

Prepare the Lemon, Garlic, and Herbes de Provence Baste: Combine the olive oil, butter, sugar, garlic, onion, oregano, lavender, rosemary, thyme, parsley, salt, black pepper, and red pepper flakes in a 2-quart saucepan and bring just to a simmer; remove from the heat. (For the best flavor, refrigerate in a tightly sealed container for 1 to 2 days and reheat over low heat to melt the butter before using.)

Using the herb brush, moisten the chicken on all sides with some of the baste. Whisk the vinegar and lemon juice into the remaining baste and set aside.

Put the chicken breast side up in the preheated skillet and smoke for 10 minutes. Turn it on its side, baste lightly, and cook for 10 minutes. Turn it onto the other side, baste lightly, and cook for another 10 minutes.

For the vegetables and herbs: Turn the chicken breast side up and scatter the vegetables and herbs around it. Cook for 20 minutes.

Add the white wine to the pan and cook for 10 minutes, or until the internal temperature of the thigh registers 160°F on an instant-read thermometer. Transfer the chicken to a platter (set the pan aside) and allow to rest for 10 to 15 minutes.

Meanwhile, boil the pan juices over medium heat until reduced to a glaze. Add the chicken stock and boil until reduced by half. Swirl in the butter piece by piece, then pass the sauce through a fine-mesh strainer into a sauceboat or small serving bowl. Stir in the chopped parsley.

Serve the chicken, whole or cut up, sprinkled with the lemon thyme salt. Pass the sauce at the table.

Basic Brine

8 cups water

1/4 cup sea or kosher salt

2 tablespoons granulated sugar

2 lemons, cut in half

3 bay leaves, preferably fresh

8 garlic cloves, crushed and peeled

2 tablespoons fresh thyme leaves

1 tablespoon black peppercorns

1 teaspoon red pepper flakes

Combine all the ingredients in a large saucepan and bring to a boil over high heat. Transfer to a bowl or other container and allow to cool, then refrigerate overnight before using.

Very Basic Brine

1/4 cup sea or kosher salt

3 cups water

2 cups apple juice

10 garlic cloves, crushed and peeled

1 tablespoon coarsely ground black pepper

Combine all the ingredients in a medium saucepan and bring to a boil over high heat. Transfer to a bowl or other container and allow to cool, then refrigerate overnight before using.

FRESH, SPRIGHTLY, AND GREEN

Think of the ingredients in these side dishes as time-release flavor capsules, meaning that you have to chew these crunch-based recipes in order to enjoy the essence within. As you bite into them, the cadence of chewing changes from simply shearing meat. The crisp and sprightly flavors mix with the barbecued meat, fish, or poultry. The light, refreshing taste and texture add high notes to the overall experience, extending the pleasure of eating. Even if you served the best, smokiest, most tender ribs in the whole city of Memphis, Tennessee, they would get boring if not complemented by a contrasting taste. So, for the relief of temporary culinary boredom, dig into the following recipes.

GREEN APPLE, CABBAGE, AND CARAWAY SLAW

SERVES 6 TO 8

Champion barbecuers often inject their creations with apple juice or slather them with apple jelly or both. So, as the saying goes, when in Rome . . .

This slaw is slightly acidic and tangy from the green apple. It has massive crunch and little flavor capsules of caraway.

6 cups finely shredded green cabbage

2 red bell peppers, cored, seeded, and thinly sliced

2 tablespoons granulated sugar

DRESSING

½ cup mayonnaise

¼ cup sour cream

¼ cup white wine vinegar

2 tablespoons finely chopped Spanish onion

1 tablespoon caraway seeds, toasted in a small skillet and finely ground

Sea or kosher salt and freshly ground black pepper to taste

4 Granny Smith apples, halved, cored, and cut into julienne (skin left on)

2 cups small watercress sprigs

2 tablespoons finely chopped shallots

2 tablespoons thinly sliced (on the bias) red chile pepper

2 tablespoons thinly sliced (on the bias) scallions

½ cup fresh dill leaves

¼ cup chopped fresh flat-leaf parsley

Combine the cabbage and bell peppers in a large bowl and mix well. Toss with the sugar and allow to macerate for 15 minutes.

Make the dressing: Combine all the ingredients in a blender and blend until smooth.

Add the apples, watercress, shallots, chile pepper, scallions, dill, and parsley to the cabbage and peppers and mix well. Toss with the dressing to coat and serve.

MANGO CILANTRO SALAD

SERVES 4 TO 6

This recipe takes inspiration from Southeast Asian flavors by combining mango, cilantro, and cucumber in a salad. The high acidity of the dressing really snaps the fat in a pork shoulder or brisket.

DRESSING
½ cup freshly squeezed lime juice
2 tablespoons Greek yogurt
¼ cup mild olive oil
Sea or kosher salt and freshly ground black pepper to taste

2 cups julienned unripe mango (about 1 large mango)

1 cup julienned ripe mango
1 cup julienned cucumber
½ cup thinly sliced red onion
¼ cup thinly sliced (on the bias) scallions
½ cup finely chopped fresh cilantro (including some stems)
2 tablespoons thinly slivered (chiffonade) fresh mint leaves

Make the dressing: Combine all the ingredients in a small bowl, mixing well.

Combine the unripe and ripe mango, cucumber, red onion, scallions, cilantro, and mint in a large bowl, tossing well. Drizzle the dressing over the salad, tossing gently, and serve.

PICKLED RAMPS

Ramps are the wild relatives of onions and garlic. And they *are* wild! Even though ramps are slightly tamed by pickling, they are still pungent but beautifully acidic and even a little sweet from the brine. They complement any collagen-rich, deeply flavored meat.

I pound ramps, green tops removed

I cup white wine vinegar

½ cup granulated sugar

I tablespoon thinly sliced fresh ginger

2 garlic cloves, crushed and peeled

I red chile pepper, preferably cayenne, seeded and cut lengthwise into 4 strips

I bay leaf, preferably fresh

I tablespoon coriander seeds

I ½ teaspoons fennel seeds

I teaspoon black peppercorns

If necessary, split larger ramps lengthwise in half so they are all about the same thickness. Blanch the ramps in boiling salted water for 10 to 15 seconds, then immediately transfer to a bowl of ice water to cool. Drain and pat dry lightly with paper towels.

Put the ramps in a canning jar that holds them loosely, and set aside.

Combine the vinegar, sugar, ginger, garlic, chile pepper, bay leaf, coriander seeds, fennel seeds, and peppercorns in a medium saucepan and bring to a simmer, stirring to dissolve the sugar.

Pour the brine over the ramps and seal the jar. Allow to cool, then refrigerate for at least 12 hours before serving. The ramps will keep for at least 5 days in the refrigerator.

RADISH AND MINT SALAD

Radishes are crunchy, bitter, peppery, and cool. Adding mint makes them grassy and even cooler.

VINAIGRETTE

- 1 tablespoon freshly squeezed lemon juice
- Sea or kosher salt and freshly ground black pepper
- 2 tablespoons mild olive oil
- 1/4 cup thinly sliced (on the bias) scallions
- 2 tablespoons thinly sliced shallots
- 1 tablespoon thinly sliced red chile pepper

- 1 cup julienned peeled daikon radish
- 1 cup quartered French breakfast radishes
- 1 cup thinly sliced red radishes
- 1 cup arugula leaves
- 1 cup julienned endive
- 3 tablespoons torn fresh mint leaves

Make the vinaigrette: Whisk together the lemon juice and salt and pepper to taste in a small bowl, then whisk in the olive oil. Whisk in the scallions, shallots, and chile pepper.

Toss all the radishes together in a medium bowl. Add the arugula, endive, and mint, tossing gently. Toss with just enough vinaigrette to coat and serve.

PEACH AND NECTARINE SALAD WITH SLIVERED ALMONDS

SERVES 4 TO 6

This salad makes for a sweet, nicely acidic complement to fattier fish such as the underappreciated bluefish. Try it with grilled sausages as well, or any cut of pork or lamb. The slivered almonds add contrasting bitterness and crunch.

2 tablespoons granulated sugar

4 peaches, halved and pitted

1 tablespoon unsalted butter

4 nectarines, halved, pitted, and cut into ⅛-inch-thick slivers

2 tablespoons finely chopped red onion

2 cups tender dandelion greens or arugula leaves

½ cup chopped fresh cilantro

2 tablespoons freshly squeezed lime juice

1 tablespoon mild olive oil

Sea or kosher salt and freshly ground black pepper

Aged balsamic vinegar for drizzling

Extra-virgin olive oil for drizzling

¼ cup toasted slivered almonds

Spread the sugar on a plate and coat the cut sides of the peaches with the sugar.

Heat a flat cast-iron griddle or large cast-iron skillet over medium-high heat until hot. Add the butter and let it melt. Add the peaches, cut side down, and cook until well caramelized on the cut surfaces, 4 to 5 minutes. Transfer to a plate.

Combine the nectarines, red onion, dandelion greens, and cilantro in a medium bowl. Add the lime juice, mild olive oil, and salt and pepper to taste and toss gently.

Mound the nectarine salad in the center of a platter and arrange the caramelized peaches, cut side up, around it. Drizzle with balsamic vinegar and extra-virgin olive oil, sprinkle with the toasted almonds, and serve.

LEMONY ASPARAGUS SHAVINGS WITH GOAT'S-MILK-CURD DRESSING

SERVES 4 TO 6

Shaving raw asparagus results in long and wafer-thin green strands, like asparagus fettuccine. The cell walls of the raw asparagus are broken and soak up dressing beautifully, slightly tenderizing the crisp asparagus but still preserving some of their pleasing snap. Creamy goat cheese provides the perfect textural counterpoint and also has enough acidity to unify the dish.

Regular goat cheese is fine, but if you are near a farmers' market that sells goat cheese, ask for the curds. They stay pristinely white in this salad, which never fails to impress guests—not to mention your own palate.

1 pound pencil asparagus, bottom ¼ inch of stalks cut off

15 to 20 thick asparagus spears, bottom ¼ inch of stalks cut off

DRESSING

1 cup (8 ounces) goat's-milk curds or 8 ounces fresh goat cheese

2 cups goat's milk or cow's milk, plus more as needed

3 tablespoons mild olive oil

2 teaspoons fresh thyme leaves

Sea or kosher salt and freshly ground black pepper

3 tablespoons finely chopped shallots

¼ cup freshly squeezed lemon juice

¼ cup extra-virgin olive oil

Sea or kosher salt and freshly ground black pepper

2 tablespoons finely chopped fresh chives

Grated zest of 2 lemons

Blanch the pencil asparagus in a large pot of boiling salted water for 1 minute. Immediately transfer to a bowl of ice water to cool, then remove from the ice water and drain on paper towels. Put in a medium bowl and set aside.

Using a vegetable peeler, shave the thick asparagus into ribbons. Transfer to another medium bowl.

Make the dressing: Put the goat's-milk curds in a large bowl and gently whisk in the milk. Whisk in the olive oil, thyme, and salt and pepper to taste. Add more milk if needed to loosen the consistency; it should be similar to that of pancake batter.

Toss the blanched asparagus with half the shallots, lemon juice, and olive oil and season with salt and pepper. Toss the shaved asparagus with the remaining shallots, lemon juice, and olive oil and season with salt and pepper.

Spoon the dressing onto individual plates, spreading it evenly. Arrange the asparagus stalks on top, followed by the asparagus shavings. Sprinkle with the chives and lemon zest and serve.

BABY BEET GREENS AND MÂCHE
WITH BALSAMIC AND SHAVED PECORINO

SERVES 8 TO 10

People often serve beets with balsamic, but for something different and more leafy/crunchy, use tender young beet greens. Don't be afraid to use those from hydroponically grown beets, as they are apt to be fresher in winter than greens grown in sunlight and shipped thousands of miles. You definitely get the savory taste of beets from their greens. Aged balsamic vinegar adds acid as it contributes beetroot color and some sweetness. The Pecorino provides umami, adding power to the flavor so that this salad can be served with any barbecued meat or chicken.

VINAIGRETTE

¼ cup champagne vinegar

1 teaspoon Dijon mustard

1 tablespoon finely chopped shallot

Sea or kosher salt and freshly ground black pepper to taste

½ cup mild extra-virgin olive oil

5 cups baby beet greens

5 cups mâche

1 cup quartered French breakfast radishes

½ cup thinly sliced red onion (cut the onion in half before slicing)

2 tablespoons aged balsamic vinegar

¼ cup aged Pecorino shavings (use a vegetable peeler)

Make the vinaigrette: Whisk all the ingredients together in a small bowl.

Combine the beet greens, mâche, radishes, and red onion in a large salad bowl and toss with just enough vinaigrette to coat. Drizzle with the balsamic, scatter the Pecorino shavings over the top, and serve.

PICKLED MIXED VEGETABLES

SERVES 4 TO 6

Crudités and dip are a time-honored way to give guests something to eat while you are waiting for the barbecue—and are great with beer. The flavors in the pickling brine for these vegetables add tang, spiced aromatic notes, and peppery heat. So simple, yet so powerful.

2 cups white wine vinegar

2 cups water

½ cup granulated sugar

3 garlic cloves, crushed and peeled

8 fresh thyme branches

¼ cup small fresh cilantro sprigs

1 tablespoon coriander seeds

1 teaspoon black peppercorns

1 cup 3-inch-long carrot batons (¼ inch thick)

1 cup halved red radishes

1 cup 1-inch cauliflower florets

2 mild red chile peppers, split and seeds removed

1 cup quartered red onions (leave enough of the root ends to keep the onion quarters intact)

½ cup ½-inch-wide red bell pepper strips

Combine all the ingredients in a large stainless steel or other nonreactive saucepan and bring to a simmer over medium heat. Cover and cook for 5 minutes. Remove from the heat and allow to cool.

Refrigerate the vegetables for at least 24 hours before serving; they will keep for 2 to 3 days, tightly covered, in the refrigerator.

CHARRED RADICCHIO WITH SWEET-AND-STICKY BALSAMIC AND BACON

SERVES 8 TO 10

Grilling radicchio's deep-red leaves to a bitter char to match the char on a piece of grilled meat creates a heavenly combination. The soft grilled leaves respond well to the sticky-sweet acidity of good balsamic vinegar. It fills the mouth with bitter sweetness. And the bacon makes it all better, because that's the great culinary virtue of smoky, fatty cured pork. It is a daydream on a plate.

DRESSING

2 tablespoons sherry vinegar

2 tablespoons finely chopped shallots

1 teaspoon red pepper flakes

1 teaspoon garlic paste (1 to 2 cloves mashed with a pinch of salt)

Pinch each of sea or kosher salt and freshly ground black pepper

2 tablespoons extra-virgin olive oil

1 teaspoon dried oregano

1 teaspoon fresh thyme leaves

¼ cup chopped fresh flat-leaf parsley

4 to 5 heads radicchio, quartered and core trimmed

16 to 20 slices bacon

2 tablespoons aged balsamic vinegar

¼ cup extra-virgin olive oil

2 tablespoons chopped fresh chives

Preheat the grill to medium-low.

Make the dressing: Whisk all the ingredients together in a small bowl.

Put the radicchio in a large bowl and drizzle with just enough dressing to coat lightly, tossing gently.

Lay a slice of bacon on a work surface and wrap a radicchio quarter tightly in the bacon, starting from the bottom end and continuing to just shy of ¼ inch from the top. Repeat with the remaining bacon and radicchio.

(continued)

Radicchio leaves aren't hydrated, unlike most other lettuces. As a result, radicchio is built to grill: it doesn't leach out water during cooking or wilt too much, and it's tong-friendly.

Put the radicchio quarters on the oiled clean grill grate and cook until crisp and golden on the first side, about 2 minutes. Turn and cook until crisp and golden on the second side, about 2 minutes, then turn and cook until crisp and golden on the third side.

Transfer the radicchio to a platter. Drizzle with the balsamic vinegar and olive oil, sprinkle with the chopped chives, and serve.

BUTTER LETTUCE SALAD
WITH POMMERY MUSTARD DRESSING

Butter lettuce, also called Bibb lettuce in America, is said to have first been grown in Kentucky, where the limestone soil accounts for the best bourbon-making water. The Pommery mustard is full of tiny mustard seeds that pop when you chew them, like caviar or tapioca or champagne grapes.

Serve with roast chicken or stronger-tasting (oily) fish, such as salmon, mackerel, or bluefish.

DRESSING

2 tablespoons Pommery mustard

¼ cup champagne vinegar

2 tablespoons finely chopped shallots

Sea or kosher salt and freshly ground black pepper to taste

¼ cup mild extra-virgin olive oil

2 to 3 medium vine-ripened or heirloom tomatoes, thinly sliced

1 teaspoon sea or kosher salt

1 teaspoon freshly ground black pepper

2 tablespoons finely chopped fresh chives

2 heads butter lettuce, leaves separated

2 tablespoons fresh dill leaves

Make the dressing: Whisk all the ingredients together in a small bowl.

Arrange the tomatoes on a large rimmed plate and season with the salt and pepper. Sprinkle with the chives. Pour the dressing over the tomatoes and let macerate for 10 minutes.

Arrange the tomatoes on a large platter, leaving the dressing on the plate.

Put the lettuce and dill in a large bowl and drizzle with the dressing, tossing gently to coat. Arrange the lettuce on top of the tomatoes and serve.

WATERCRESS WITH PICKLED GARLIC AND SMOKED ANCHOVIES

The names of the ingredients pretty much tell the tale: this recipe screams flavor.

Somewhere in the process of pickling the garlic cloves, the brine takes away all the sharpness. Once it's been tamed by the brine, you can eat garlic to your heart's content and still have a social life with those who don't worship this divine bulb. You have to try it for yourself. Pickled garlic cloves and smoked anchovies are available in some Spanish markets, at gourmet shops, or online (see Sources, page 91).

VINAIGRETTE

Juice of 1 lemon

1 teaspoon sherry vinegar

1 tablespoon finely chopped shallot

2 tablespoons extra-virgin olive oil

Sea or kosher salt and freshly ground black pepper to taste

¼ cup halved pickled garlic cloves

16 to 20 smoked anchovy fillets, cut lengthwise into 3 strips each (or substitute anchovies packed in olive oil)

¼ cup finely diced jarred piquillo peppers

5 to 6 cups watercress sprigs

¼ cup fresh flat-leaf parsley leaves

1 tablespoon fresh marjoram leaves

Make the vinaigrette: Whisk all the ingredients together in a small bowl.

Transfer 2 tablespoons of the vinaigrette to a large bowl and add the pickled garlic, anchovies, and diced peppers, tossing to coat. Add the watercress and herbs and toss lightly, adding just enough vinaigrette to coat. Serve.

WARM CRUNCHY BROCCOLINI WITH PROSCIUTTO AND SCRUFFED CROUTONS

SERVES 4 TO 6

Just as winter and its best caramelized root vegetables and braised cabbage have ceased to hold any allure, Broccolini arrives in the market like a bright green promise of the coming season's fresh bounty. It can become strong tasting as the season wears on, but at this time of year it has just the right amount of slight bitterness and doesn't require long cooking. A quick blanching does the trick but leaves it fresh and crunchy. Finish with roughly cut croutons and strips of prosciutto for a salad packed with flavor. Serve with anything grilled—or add some cheese and charcuterie for a light stand-alone meal.

VINAIGRETTE

2 tablespoons finely chopped shallots

I teaspoon Colman's dry mustard

½ teaspoon granulated sugar

Juice of 2 lemons

2 tablespoons white wine vinegar

I tablespoon finely chopped red chile pepper, such as cayenne

½ teaspoon red pepper flakes, soaked in I tablespoon boiling water (to bring out the flavor)

Sea or kosher salt and freshly ground black pepper to taste

¾ cup extra-virgin olive oil

4 cups I-inch pieces Broccolini (florets and stems)

CROUTONS

3 tablespoons unsalted butter

3 tablespoons extra-virgin olive oil

2 cups torn rustic Italian bread (approximately ½-inch pieces)

5 garlic cloves, crushed and peeled

2 tablespoons fresh rosemary leaves

4 ounces thinly sliced (⅛-inch-thick) prosciutto, cut into ⅛-inch-wide strips

I teaspoon garlic salt

I teaspoon freshly ground black pepper

Sea or kosher salt and freshly ground black pepper, if necessary

Extra-virgin olive oil for drizzling

2 lemons, cut in half

Make the vinaigrette: Whisk all the ingredients together in a small bowl. Set aside.

Blanch the Broccolini in a large pot of boiling salted water for 3 minutes. Drain and immediately transfer to a bowl of ice water to cool. Remove from the ice water and drain on paper towels.

Prepare the croutons: Combine the butter and olive oil in a skillet large enough to hold the pieces of bread in a single layer and heat until crackling. Add the bread, garlic, and rosemary, stirring to coat the bread, and cook, stirring and shaking the pan, until the croutons are golden brown. Remove from the heat, add the prosciutto, tossing to mix, and season with the garlic salt and pepper. Transfer to a plate and allow to cool.

To serve, toss the Broccolini with the vinaigrette and adjust the seasoning with salt and pepper if necessary. Arrange on a platter and scatter the croutons over the top. Drizzle with a little olive oil and garnish the platter with the lemon halves.

BELGIAN ENDIVE SALAD WITH BURNT ORANGES, MARJORAM DRESSING, AND POMEGRANATE SEEDS

SERVES 8 TO 10

When oranges are halved and cooked on a griddle, or plancha, the result is burnt (but not to the point of bitter carbonization) on the cooked side and then progressively less cooked as you eat your way through them. It makes for a very interesting taste narrative.

Endives add watery crunch. The crowning touch is marjoram, an herb not frequently used in the United States. It's like a pungent cross between oregano and rosemary, only more floral, and marjoram seems to retain its highly flavorful oils more than oregano or rosemary. A food scientist would say the oils don't volatilize as readily, but you don't need science to know and appreciate the flavor. It works particularly well with bitter greens.

¼ cup granulated sugar

4 to 5 oranges, peel and all white pith removed, cut in half

¼ cup fresh marjoram leaves

DRESSING

3 tablespoons champagne vinegar

1 tablespoon finely chopped shallot

1 tablespoon crème fraîche or Greek yogurt

Sea or kosher salt and freshly ground black pepper to taste

3 tablespoons mild extra-virgin olive oil

6 to 8 Belgian endives, cut lengthwise in half, cored, and cut on the bias into 1-inch-wide pieces

2 tablespoons ½-inch batons fresh chives

Seeds from 2 pomegranates

Spread the sugar on a large plate and put the oranges cut side down on the sugar.

Heat a griddle or large cast-iron pan over high heat until it just starts to smoke. Pierce an orange half with a fork and transfer to the hot pan,

sugar side down; repeat with the remaining oranges. Cook until the cut surfaces of the oranges are deeply caramelized, about 2 minutes. Transfer the oranges, cut side up, to a platter and sprinkle with the marjoram. Set aside.

Make the dressing: Whisk all the ingredients together in a small bowl.

Put the endive in a large bowl and toss with just enough dressing to coat lightly. Transfer to a platter, arrange the caramelized oranges around the endive, sprinkle with the chive batons and pomegranate seeds, and serve.

ARUGULA SALAD WITH LEMON, EXTRA-VIRGIN OLIVE OIL, AND PARMESAN SHAVINGS

SERVES 8 TO 10

There may be no simpler recipe in this book, but its clarity of flavor and texture plays consummate counterpoint to the densely layered notes of meat, herbs, salt, and smoke. The strong mouth-puckering acidity of cut-up lemon segments breaks the mouth-coating effect of fat like a slap of bay rum on your face after a shave. Baby or young arugula is the way to go. The arugula should be slightly bitter to encourage the tasting process to come to a halt, which can then start anew with the next bite, but super-bitter, mature arugula is unpleasant. For a seasonal change, substitute dandelion greens for the arugula, as pictured.

VINAIGRETTE
Juice of 2 lemons
1 tablespoon white wine vinegar
1/4 teaspoon granulated sugar
Sea or kosher salt and freshly ground black pepper to taste
1/4 cup extra-virgin olive oil

2 lemons
10 cups arugula leaves
1/4 cup fresh flat-leaf parsley leaves
1/4 cup fresh dill leaves
1/4 cup 1/2-inch batons fresh chives
1/4 cup Parmesan shavings (use a vegetable peeler)

Make the vinaigrette: Whisk all the ingredients together in a small bowl. Set aside.

Using a sharp serrated or other knife, cut off the top and bottom of each lemon to expose the flesh. Stand each lemon up on the cutting board and carefully cut away the skin and bitter white pith in strips, working from top to bottom and following the natural curve of the fruit. Trim away any remaining pith.

(continued)

To remove the lemon segments (suprêmes), work over a bowl and cut down along the membranes on either side of each section to release it, letting the sections drop into the bowl as you go. Cut each segment crosswise in half.

Combine the arugula, parsley, and dill in a large salad bowl. Add the lemon segments, then toss gently with just enough vinaigrette to coat. Scatter the chive batons and Parmesan shavings over the top and serve.

Sources

D'Artagnan
dartagnan.com
Duck fat, magrets (duck breasts),
venison, and other meats and game

ImportFood
importfood.com
A vast selection of Thai ingredients,
including whole pickled garlic

JB Prince
jbprince.com
Knives and other high-quality
kitchen equipment

La Tienda
tienda.com
Jarred piquillo peppers, smoked
anchovies, and other Spanish
ingredients

Microplane
microplane.com
High-quality graters and zesters

Niman Ranch
nimanranch.com
Free-range and organic meats

Penzey's Spices
penzeys.com
Sea salt, juniper berries, and a vast
range of other spices

Sur La Table
surlatable.com
Dehydrators and other kitchen
equipment of all kinds

Weber
weber.com
Grills and accessories

Index

Note: Page numbers in *italics* refer to illustrations.

Conversion Charts

Here are rounded-off equivalents between the metric system and the traditional systems that are used in the United States to measure weight and volume.

FRACTIONS	DECIMALS
⅛	.125
¼	.25
⅓	.33
⅜	.375
½	.5
⅝	.625
⅔	.67
¾	.75
⅞	.875

WEIGHTS

US/UK	METRIC
¼ oz	7 g
½ oz	15 g
1 oz	30 g
2 oz	55 g
3 oz	85 g
4 oz	110 g
5 oz	140 g
6 oz	170 g
7 oz	200 g
8 oz (½ lb)	225 g
9 oz	250 g
10 oz	280 g
11 oz	310 g
12 oz	340 g
13 oz	370 g
14 oz	400 g
15 oz	425 g
16 oz (1 lb)	450 g

VOLUME

AMERICAN	IMPERIAL	METRIC
¼ tsp		1.25 ml
½ tsp		2.5 ml
1 tsp		5 ml
½ Tbsp (1½ tsp)		7.5 ml
1 Tbsp (3 tsp)		15 ml
¼ cup (4 Tbsp)	2 fl oz	60 ml
⅓ cup (5 Tbsp)	2½ fl oz	75 ml
½ cup (8 Tbsp)	4 fl oz	125 ml
⅔ cup (10 Tbsp)	5 fl oz	150 ml
¾ cup (12 Tbsp)	6 fl oz	175 ml
1 cup (16 Tbsp)	8 fl oz	250 ml
1¼ cups	10 fl oz	300 ml
1½ cups	12 fl oz	350 ml
2 cups (1 pint)	16 fl oz	500 ml
2½ cups	20 fl oz (1 pint)	625 ml
5 cups	40 fl oz (1 qt)	1.25 l

OVEN TEMPERATURES

	°F	°C	GASMARK
Very cool	250–275	130–140	½–1
Cool	300	148	2
Warm	325	163	3
Moderate	350	177	4
Moderately hot	375–400	190–204	5–6
Hot	425	218	7
Very hot	450–475	232–245	8–9

Library of Congress Cataloging-in-Publication Data

Names: Lang, Adam Perry, author. | Kaminsky, Peter, author.
Title: The artisanal kitchen : barbecue sides / Adam Perry Lang with Peter Kaminsky.
Other titles: Barbecue sides
Description: New York : Artisan, a division of Workman Publishing Co., Inc. [2021] | Includes index.
Identifiers: LCCN 2020007325 | ISBN 9781579659837 (hardcover)
Subjects: LCSH: Barbecuing. | Side dishes (Cooking)
Classification: LCC TX840.B3 L38 2021 | DDC 641.76—dc23
LC record available at https://lccn.loc.gov/2020007325

Cover and interior design by Suet Chong

Artisan books are available at special discounts when purchased in bulk for premiums and sales promotions as well as for fund-raising or educational use. Special editions or book excerpts also can be created to specification. For details, contact the Special Sales Director at the address below, or send an e-mail to specialmarkets@workman.com.

For speaking engagements, contact speakersbureau@workman.com.

Published by Artisan
A division of Workman Publishing Co., Inc.
225 Varick Street
New York, NY 10014-4381
artisanbooks.com

Artisan is a registered trademark of Workman Publishing Co., Inc.

This book has been adapted from *Charred & Scruffed* (Artisan, 2012).

Published simultaneously in Canada by Thomas Allen & Son, Limited

Printed in China

First printing, March 2021

10 9 8 7 6 5 4 3 2 1